BIOGRAPHY OF MUGHAL EMPERORS

SHIVAM

ISBN 979-888530504-4

Thanks for Purchasing this book

In this book you will get the full Biography of all the importent

Mughal Emperors.

This book is Divided in 7 chapters

Chapter 1 --> Babur

Chapter 2 --> Humayun

Chapter 3 --> Akbar the Great

Chapter 4 --> Jahangir

Chapter 5 --> shah jahan

Chapter 6 --> Aurangzeb

Chapter 7 --> bahadur shah zafar ll

Contents

I
Babur

Babur: The founder of Mughal Empire

Babur, (Persian: "Tiger") also spelled Babar or Bāber, original name Ẓahir al-Din Muḥammad, (born February 15, 1483, principality of Fergana [now in Uzbekistan]—died December 26, 1530, Agra [India]), emperor (1526–30) and founder of the Mughal dynasty of northern India. Bābur, a descendant of the Mongol conqueror Genghis Khan and also of the Turkic conqueror Timur (Tamerlane), was a military adventurer, a soldier of distinction, and a poet and diarist of genius, as well as a statesman.

Early years

Babur came from the Barlas tribe of Mongol origin, but isolated members of the tribe considered themselves Turks in language and customs through long residence in Turkish regions. Hence, Babur, though called a Mughal, drew most of his support from Turks, and the empire he founded was Turkish in character. His family had become members of the Chagatai clan, by which name they are known. He was fifth in male succession from Timur and 13th through the female line from Genghis Khan. Bābur's father, 'Umar Shaykh Mīrzā, ruled the small principality of Fergana to the north of the Hindu Kush mountain range. Because there was no fixed law of succession among the Turks, every prince of the Timurids—the dynasty founded by Timur—considered it his right to rule the whole of Timur's dominions. Those territories were vast, and, hence, the princes' claims led to unending wars. The Timurid princes, moreover, considered themselves kings by profession, their business being to rule others without observing too precisely whether any particular region had actually formed a part of Timur's empire. Bābur's father, true to that tradition, spent his life trying to recover Timur's old capital of Samarkand (now in Uzbekistan), and Bābur followed in his footsteps. The qualities needed to succeed in that dynastic warfare were the abilities to inspire loyalty and devotion, to manage the turbulent factions often caused by family feuds, and to draw revenue from the trading and agricultural classes. Bābur eventually mastered them all, but he was also a commander of genius.

For 10 years (1494–1504) Bābur sought to recover Samarkand and twice occupied it briefly (in 1497 and 1501). But in Muḥammad Shaybānī Khan, a descendant of Genghis Khan and ruler of the Uzbeks beyond the Jaxartes River (ancient name for the Syr Darya), he had an opponent more powerful than even his closest relatives. In 1501 Bābur was decisively defeated at Sar-e Pol and within three years had lost both Samarkand and his principality of Fergana. There was always hope at that time, however, for a prince with engaging qualities and strong leadership abilities. In 1504 Bābur seized Kabul (Afghanistan) with his personal followers, maintaining himself there against all rebellions and intrigues. His last unsuccessful attempt on Samarkand (1511–12) induced him to give up a futile quest and to concentrate on expansion elsewhere. In 1522, when he was already turning his attention to Sindh (now a province in Pakistan) and India, he finally secured Kandahār, a strategic site (now in Afghanistan) on the road to Sindh.

When Bābur made his first raid into India in 1519, the Punjab region (now divided between the Indian state and the Pakistani province) was part of the dominions of Sultan Ibrāhīm Lodī of Delhi, but the governor, Dawlat Khan Lodī, resented Ibrāhīm's attempts to diminish his authority. By 1524 Bābur had invaded the Punjab three more times but was unable to master the tangled course of Punjab and Delhi politics sufficiently enough to achieve a firm foothold. Yet it was clear that the Delhi sultanate was involved in contentious quarreling and ripe for overthrow. After mounting a full-scale attack there, Bābur was recalled by an Uzbek attack on his Kabul kingdom, but a joint request for help from ʿĀlam Khan, Ibrāhīm's uncle, and Dawlat Khan encouraged Bābur to attempt his fifth, and first successful, raid.

Major successes

Victories in India

Setting out in November 1525, Bābur met Ibrāhīm at Panipat, 50 miles (80 km) north of Delhi, on April 21, 1526. Bābur's army was estimated at no more than 12,000, but they were seasoned followers, adept at cavalry tactics, and were aided by new artillery acquired from the Ottoman Turks. Ibrāhīm's army was said to number 100,000 with 100 elephants, but its tactics were antiquated and it was dissentious. Bābur won the battle by coolness under fire, his use of artillery, and effective Turkish wheeling tactics on a divided, dispirited enemy. Ibrāhīm was killed in battle. With his usual speed, Bābur occupied Delhi three days later and reached Agra on May 4. His first action there was to lay out a garden, now known as the Ram Bagh, by the Yamuna (Jumna) River.

Babur's MosqueBabur's Mosque, Panipat, northwestern India.

That brilliant success must have seemed at the time to be of little difference from one of his former forays on Samarkand. His small force, burdened by the oppressive weather and located 800 miles (1,300 km) from their base at Kabul, was surrounded by powerful foes. All down the Ganges (Ganga) River valley were militant Afghan chiefs, in disarray but with a formidable military potential. To the south were the kingdoms of Malwa and Gujarat, both with extensive resources, while in Rajasthan Rana Sanga of Mewar (Udaipur) was head of a powerful confederacy threatening the whole Muslim position in northern India. Bābur's first problem was that his own followers, suffering from the heat and disheartened by the hostile surroundings, wished to return home as Timur had done. By employing threats, reproaches, promises, and appeals, vividly described in his memoirs, Bābur diverted them. He then dealt with Rana Sanga, who, when he found that Bābur was not retiring as his Turkish ancestor had done, advanced with an estimated 100,000 horses and 500 elephants. With most of the neighbouring strongholds still held by his foes, Bābur was virtually surrounded. He sought divine favour by abjuring liquor, breaking the wine vessels and pouring the wine down a well. His followers responded both to that act and his stirring exhortations and stood their ground at Khanua, 37 miles (60 km) west of Agra, on March 16, 1527. Bābur used his customary tactics—a barrier of wagons for his centre, with gaps for the artillery and for cavalry sallies, and wheeling cavalry charges on the wings. The artillery stamped the elephants, and the flank charges bewildered the Rajputs (ruling warrior caste), who, after 10 hours, broke, never to rally under a single leader again.

Bābur now had to deal with the defiant Afghans to the east, who had captured Lucknow while he was facing Rana Sanga. Other Afghans had rallied to Sultan Ibrāhīm's brother Maḥmūd Lodī, who had occupied Bihar. There were also Rajput chiefs still defying him, principally the ruler of Chanderi. After capturing that fortress in January 1528, Bābur turned to the east. Crossing the Ganges, he drove the Afghan captor of Lucknow into Bengal. He then turned on Maḥmūd Lodī, whose army was scattered in Bābur's third great victory, that of the Ghaghara, where that river joins the Ganges, on May 6, 1529. Artillery was again decisive, helped by the skillful handling of boats.

Establishment of the Mughal Empire

Bābur's dominions were now secure from Kandahār to the borders of Bengal, with a southern limit marked by the Rajput desert and the forts of Ranthambhor, Gwalior, and Chanderi. Within that great area, however, there was no settled administration, only a congeries of quarreling chiefs. An empire had been gained but still had to be pacified and organized. It was thus a precarious heritage that Bābur passed on to his son Humāyūn.

In 1530, when Humāyūn became deathly ill, Bābur is said to have offered his life to God in exchange for Humāyūn's, walking seven times around the bed to complete the vow. Humāyūn recovered and Bābur's health declined, and Bābur died the same year.

Legacy

Bābur is rightly considered the founder of the Mughal Empire, even though the work of consolidating the empire was performed by his grandson Akbar. Bābur, moreover, provided the magnetic leadership that inspired the next two generations

Bābur was a military adventurer of genius and an empire builder of good fortune, with an engaging personality. He was also a gifted Turki poet, which would have won him distinction apart from his political career, as well as a lover of nature who constructed gardens wherever he went and complemented beautiful spots by holding convivial parties. Finally, his prose memoirs, the Bābur-nāmeh, have become a renowned autobiography. They were translated from Turki into Persian in Akbar's reign (1589), were translated into English, Memoirs of Bābur, in two volumes, and were first published in 1921–22. They portray a ruler unusually magnanimous for his age, cultured, and witty, with an adventurous spirit and an acute eye for natural beauty.

II
Humayun

Humayun the second Mughal emperor

Humayun is the second Mughal emperor, the dynasty ruling North India from the sixteenth to the nineteenth century. He is the great-grandfather of Shah Jahan, the builder of the Taj Mahal. Heir to a new and particularly unstable empire, he will have to fight two successive rebellions, lose his throne and will be able to reconstitute his father's empire only after fifteen years of progress, going from battle to battle. He will leave his son a larger Empire than he has received, from Afghanistan to Bengal.

The Early years

Humayun was born on March 17, 1508 in Kabul, during a period when his father, Bâbur, was trying to expand his kingdom. He followed him in his wanderings throughout his childhood and, at the age of 18, he was at his side during the battle of Pânipat (1526), a founding battle of the Mughal Empire. Then he participated in the capture of Agra and was sent to pacify the valley of the Ganges, in the far east of the Empire. In 1528 he received the governorate of Badakhshan, a region now straddling between South Tajikistan and North Afghanistan. It is also south of Ferghana, the original kingdom of the dynasty, and east of Kabul, a city that served as a rear base for the conquests of Babur and which represents the starting point of the dynasty. Badakhshan was a bit like the original territory of the Empire.

Accession to the throne

Humâyûn ascends the throne after his father's death in 1530. Since his Empire is not yet stabilized rebellions are close and are triggered very shortly thereafter. He had to face two foci of rebellion: that of Bahâdûr Shâh, Goujerat and that of Sher Shâh Sûrî in Bihar.

Goujerat is the most northern region of the west coast of India, bordering Pakistan. Bahâdûr Shâh was the local Sultan and had to face at once the virtues of the conquest of Humâyûn and the attacks of the Portuguese, newcomers from Europe wishing to reign over part of the lands of India to promote trade. Bahâdûr Shâh therefore raised an army and marched towards Delhi. To counter it Humâyûn came to the Kalinjar fortress in 1531 and sieged it until he obtained a large ransom, which enabled him to finance troops for years to come. He then leaves for the second rebel home, Bihar, in the east of the country, near Bengal. There it is Sher Shâh Sûrî who poses a problem.

Sher Shâh Sûrî was an Afghan leader who had a great climb. Entering the service of the Sultan of Bihar in 1522 he served Bâbur in 1527 and 1528, which rewarded him by granting him land. Not accommodating himself he goes to conquer Bihar, joins the Sultant of Bengal and founds an independent kingdom. It is at this moment that Humayyun worries about the eastern part of his Empire, nibbled by this former ally. Once the campaign of Goujerat finished he then takes the path of Bihar but instead of going to the capital, Gaur, he believed free, he sieges the city of Chunar, allowing time for his enemy to take Gaur.

Humâyûn then took the road to Gaur and laid siege to that city in order to regain his authority over Bihar and then Bengal, but in the meantime Sher Shâh Sûrî went west and conquered various lands within the city. the Mughal Empire, threatening Agra, the capital. As a result, the Emperor retraced his steps, but was defeated at the Battle of Buxar in June 1539. He lost his troops and his harem on this occasion and had to live only on luck.

In 1540 he reformed a new army and resumed the leadership of Bihar to fight Sher Shâh Sûrî who eventually created a kingdom over the north-east of India, but the battle that began was lost (1540,Kanauj). Humayun had to flee, first to Punjab, then to Sindh, the southern region of Pakistan.

Map of Humayun conquests

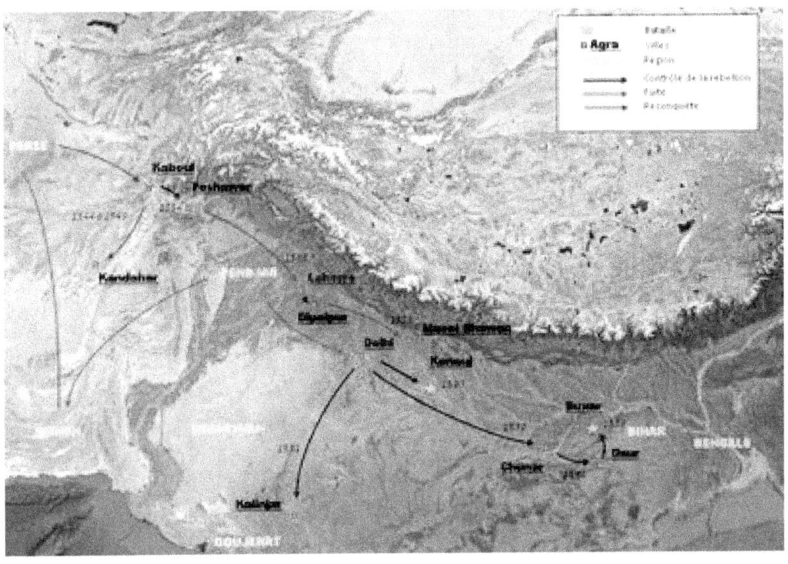

Map of Humâyûn conquests between 1530 and 1555

The recovery of the Empire

It was in Sindh that a Humayun time was installed, exiled. His son was born there in 1542. In 1544 he went to Persia to negotiate an army with Shah Tahmasp I, which he granted him. At the head of this army he first took the direction of Kandahar, then Kabul, in the hands of his brother Kâmran. The two brothers took Kabul each twice between 1544 and 1549, the last word coming back to Humâyûn who made his brother's eyes burst. Then begins the reconquest of the Mughal Empire, battle after battle: 1554 (Peshawar), 1555 (Lahore, then Dipalpur and finally Macchi Bhawan). It was this last victory in Macchi Bhawan, against the Afghans, that allowed him to return to the throne of Agra, after 15 years of exile.

Having managed to reclaim his kingdom he moved to Agra and began to structure the territory. Unfortunately a bad fall made January 27, 1556 took his life. His wife made him build a mausoleum in Delhi, on the Mughal model.

The heritage of Humayun

Tomb of Humayun

The journeys of Humayun and his father Babur are very similar to the extent that they inherited a territory, enlarged it by military conquests, were exiled and reconquered their territories by force, but died before they could organize the Empire. the successor of Humâyûn, Akbar, inherited a disparate empire, newly conquered and unstable. He also received a tradition of conquest, a nomadic lifestyle and a desire to keep the Empire at all costs.

The intangible heritage is more tenuous to the extent that it has not been able to develop the arts, organize daily life or really ruled over its Empire, so make choices that would have marked generations to come. His son Akbar will do it. It should be noted that although he is a Muslim he was neither really practicing nor a preacher, the other religions having been able to practice their cults without any problem. Linguistically, he kept the use of Chaghatai, a language derived from Turkish strongly orientated during the time of his father and his grandfather.

III
Akbar the Great

EnAbu'l-Fath Jalal ud-din Muhammad Akbar

Full Name: Abu'l-Fath Jalal ud-din Muhammad Akbar
Dynasty: Timurid; Mughal
Predecessor: Humayun
Successor: Jahangir
Coronation: February 14, 1556
Reign: February 14, 1556 – October 27, 1605
Date of Birth: October 15, 1542

Parents: Humayun (Father) and Hamida Banu Begum (Mother)

Religion: Islam (Sunni); Din-i-Ilahi

Spouse: 36 chief wives and 3 chief consorts - Ruqaiya Sultan Begum, Heera Kunwari and Salima Sultan Begum

Children: Hassan, Hussain, Jahangir, Murad, Daniyal, Aram Banu Begum, Shakr-un-Nissa Begum, Khanum Sultan Begum.

Biography: Akbarnama; Ain-i-Akbari

Mausoleum : Sikandra, Agra

Jalaluddin Muhammad Akbar, more famously known as Akbar the Great, was the third emperor of the Mughal Empire, after Babur and Humayun. He was the son of Nasiruddin Humayun and succeeded him as the emperor in the year 1556, at the tender age of just 13. Succeeding his father Humayun at a critical stage, he slowly enlarged the extent of the Mughal Empire to include almost all of the Indian sub-continent. He extended his power and influence over the entire country due to his military, political, cultural, and economic dominance. He established a centralised system of administration and adopted a policy of marriage alliance and diplomacy. With his religious policies, he won the support of his non-Muslim subjects as well. He was one of the greatest emperors of the Mughal dynasty and extended his patronage to art and culture. Being fond of literature, he extended support to literature in several languages. **Akbar**, thus, laid the foundations for a multicultural empire during his reign.

Early Life & Childhood

Akbar was born as Abu'l-Fath Jalal ud-din Muhammad at the Umerkot fort in Sind on October 15, 1542. His father Humayun, the second emperor of the Mughal dynasty was in flight after his defeat in the battle of Kanauj (in May 1540) at the hands of Sher Shah Suri. He and his wife Hamida Banu Begum, who was pregnant at that time, was granted refuge by the Hindu ruler Rana Prasad. As Humayun was in exile and had to move constantly, Akbar was brought up at the household of his paternal uncles, Kamran Mirza and Aksari Mirza. Growing up he learnt how to hunt and fight using various weapons, shaping up to be the great warrior who would be the greatest emperor of India. He never learned to read and write during his childhood, but that did not diminish his thirst for knowledge. He would often ask to be read about art and religion.

In 1555, Humayun recaptured Delhi with the military support of the Persian ruler Shah Tahmasp I. Humayun met his untimely demise soon after he reclaimed his throne after an accident. Akbar was 13 years old at that time and Humayun's trusted general Bairam Khan took up the post of Regent for the young Emperor. Akbar succeeded Humayun on February 14, 1556 in Kalanaur (Punjab) and was proclaimed 'Shahanshah'. Bairam Khan ruled on behalf of the young Emperor till he came of age.

Akbar married his cousin Ruqaiya Sultan Begum, daughter of his paternal uncle Hindal Mirza, in November 1551. Ruqaiya became his chief consort after he ascended the throne.

Quest for Power: Second Battle of Panipat

At the time of his ascent to the Mughal throne, Akbar's empire encompassed Kabul, Kandahar, Delhi and parts of Punjab. But the Afghan Sultan Mohammad Adil Shah of Chunar had designs on the throne of India and planned to wage war against the Mughals. His Hindu general Samrat Hem Chandra Vikramaditya or Hemu in short, led the Afghan army to capture Agra and Delhi soon after Humayun's death in 1556. The Mughal Army faced a humiliating defeat and they soon receded with their leader, Commander Tardi Baig absconding. Hemu ascended the throne on October 7, 1556 and established Hindu rule in North India after 350 years of Muslim Imperialism.

On the direction of his regent Bairam Khan, Akbar declared his intentions to reclaim his rights to the throne at Delhi. The Mughal forces moved to Panipat through Thaneshwar and faced Hemu's army on November 5, 1556. Hemu's army was much larger in size than of that of Akbar's with 30,000 horsemen and 1500 war elephants and he had the support of native Hindu and Afghan rulers who considered the Mughals as outsiders. Bairam Khan led the Mughal army from the back and placed skilled generals on the front, left and right flanks. Young Akbar was kept at a safe distance by his regent. Initially Hemu's army was in a better position, but a sudden change in tactics by Bairam Khan and another general Ali Quli Khan, managed to overpower the enemy army. Hemu was on an elephant when he was struck by an arrow to his eye and his elephant driver took his injured master away from the battlefield. Mughal soldiers pursued Hemu, captured him and brought him before Akbar. When asked to behead the enemy leader, Akbar could not do this and Bairam Khan executed Hemu on his behalf, thus establishing victory of the Mughals conclusively.

Crushing the Opposition

The Second battle of Panipat marked the beginning of the Glory days for the Mughal reign in India. Akbar sought out to end Afghan sovereignties that might be claimant for the throne in Delhi. Hemu's relatives were captured and imprisoned by Bairam Khan. Sher Shah's successor, Sikander Shah Sur was driven out from North India to Bihar and was subsequently compelled to surrender in 1557. Another Afghan contender to the throne, Muhammed Adil was killed in a battle the same year. Others were compelled to flee Delhi and neighbouring regions to seek refuge in other states.

Military Expansions

Akbar dedicated the first decade of his rule towards expanding his empire. Under the regency of Bairam Khan, Ajmer, Malwa and Garhkatanga were annexed into the Mughal territories. He also captured Lahore and Multan, major centers of Punjab. Ajmer brought him the doorway to Rajputana. He also claimed the Gwalior fort from the Sur Rulers. He conquered Gondwana in 1564 from the minor ruler Raja Vir Narayan. Akbar's forces met a formidable opponent in the young King's mother, Rani Durgavati, a Rajput warrior queen. On being defeated Durgavati committed suicide while Vir Narayan was slain during the capture of Chauragarh fortress.

Having consolidated his supremacy over most of north and central India, Akbar turned his attention towards Rajputana, which presented a formidable threat to his supremacy. He had already established his rule over Ajmer and Nagor. Beginning in 1561, Akbar started his quest to conquer Rajputana. He employed force as well as diplomatic tactics to make the Rajput rulers submit to his Rule. Most accepted his sovereignty except the Sisodia ruler of Mewar, Udai Singh. This presented a problem for Akbar on his designs to establish unquestioned supremacy over the region. In 1567, Akbar attacked the Chittorgarh fort in Mewar that represented a key strategic importance towards establishing rule in Rajputana. Udai Singh's chiefs Jaimal and Patta held off the Mughal forces for four months in 1568. Udai Singh was banished to the Hills of Mewar. Other Rajput states like Ranthambore fell in the face of Mughal forces, but Rana Prapat, Udai Singh's son, put up a formidable resistance to Akbar's expansion of power. He was the last of the Rajput defenders and fought till his heroic end in the Battle of Haldighati in 1576.

Following his victory over the Rajputana, Akbar brought in Gujarat (1584), Kabul (1585), Kashmir (1586-87), Sindh (1591), Bengal (1592) and Kandahar (1595) within the Mughal territory. The Mughal army led by General Mir Mausam also conquered parts of Baluchistan around Quetta and Makran by 1595.

In 1593, Akbar set out to conquer Deccan territories. He faced opposition to his authority in Ahmadnagar and attacked the Deccan state in 1595. Chand Bibi, the regent queen offered formidable opposition, but was forced to concede defeat ultimately having to give up Berar. By 1600, Akbar had captured Burhanpur, Asirgarh Fort and Khandesh.

Administration

After consolidating the empire, Akbar concentrated on establishing a stable and subject-friendly administration at the center to govern his vast empire. The principles of Akbar's administration were based on moral as well as material welfare of his subjects. He brought about several changes in existing policies to establish an environment of uniform opportunities to people irrespective of religion.

The Emperor himself was the supreme governor of the empire. He retained ultimate judicial, legislative and administrative power above anyone else. He was assisted in efficient governance by several ministers – Vakil, chief adviser to the King over all matters; Diwan, minister in charge of finance; Sadar-i-sadur, religious advisor to the King; Mir Bakshi, the one who maintained all records; Daroga-i-Dak Chowki and Muhtasib were appointed to oversee proper enforcement of law as well as the postal department.

The entire empire was divided into 15 Subas, each province being governed by a Subadar along with other regional post mirroring that in the center. The Subas were divided into Sarkars which were further divided into Parganas. The head of the Sarkar was a Faujdar and that of a Pargana was a Shikdar. Echa Pargana consisted of several villages which were governed by a Muqaddam, a Patwari and a Chowkidar, along with a panchayat.

He introduced the Mansabdari system to effectively organize the Military. The Mansabdars were responsible for maintaining discipline and impart training to the soldiers. There were 33 ranks of Mansabdars with 10,000 to 10 soldiers under their command according to rank. Akbar also introduced the custom of taking roll of the soldiers and branding of horses. Akbar's military consisted of several division viz. cavalry, infantry, elephants, artillery and navy. The emperor maintained ultimate control over the military and excelled in the ability to enforce discipline among his troops.

Land revenue was the chief source of income for the Mughal Government and Akbar introduced several reforms in the revenue department. The land was divided into four classes according to their productivity - Polaj, Parauti, Chachar and Banjar. Bigha was the unit of land measurement and land revenue was paid either in cash or in kind. Akbar on the advice of his Finance Minister Todar Mall, introduced loans against small interest to the farmers and he also granted remission of revenues in case of natural calamities like draughts or floods. He also issued special instruction to the revenue collectors to be friendly with the farmers. All these reforms greatly increased productivity and revenue of the Mughal Empire, leading to prosperous subjects with abundance of food.

Akbar introduced reforms in judicial system as well and for the first time, Hindu customs and laws were referred to in case of Hindu subjects. The Emperor was the highest authority in Law and the power to give capital punishment rested solely with him. The major social reform introduced by Akbar was the abolition of the Pilgrimage Tax for Hindus in 1563 as well as the Jazia tax imposed on the Hindu subjects. He discouraged child marriage and encouraged widow remarriage.

Diplomacy

Akbar was probably the first Islamic ruler in India who sought stable political alliances through matrimony. He married several Hindu Princess including Jodha Bai, from the house of Jaipur, Heer Kunwari from the house of Amber, and princess from the houses of Jaisalmer and Bikaner. He strengthened the alliances by welcoming male relatives of his wives as part of his court and bestowing them with important roles in his administration. Political significance of these alliances was far-reaching for the Mughal Empire in securing strong loyalty of these dynasties. This practice brought the Hindu and Muslim nobilities in close contact securing a better secular environment for the empire. The Rajput alliances became strongest allies of Akbar's army which proved crucial in many of his subsequent conquests like that in Gujarat in 1572.

Akbar and the Uzbeks of Central Asia entered into a treaty of mutual respect under which the Mughals were not to interfere in Badakshan and Balkh regions and the Uzbeks would stay away from Kandahar and Kabul. His attempt to make alliance with the newly arrived Portuguese tradesman proved futile with the Portuguese refuting his friendly advances. Another contributing factor was Emperor Akbar's relations with the Ottoman Empire. He was in regular correspondence with Ottoman Sultan Suleiman the Magnificent. His contingent of pilgrims to Mecca and Medina were warmly welcomed by the Ottoman Sultan and the Mughal Ottoman trade flourished during his rule. Akbar also continued to maintain excellent diplomatic relationship with the Safavid rulers of Persia, which dated back to his father's days with Shah Tahmasp I lending his military support to

Humayun for recapturing Delhi.

Akbar's Religious Policy

Akbar's rule was marked by wide religious tolerance and liberal outlook. Akber was profoundly religious himself, yet he never sought to enforce his own religious views on anyone; be it prisoners of war, or Hindu wives or the common people in his kingdom. He gave great importance to choice and abolished discriminatory taxes based on religion. He encouraged building of temples and even churches his empire. Out of reverence for the Hindu members of the Royal Family he banned the cooking of beef in the kitchens. Akbar became a follower of the great Sufi mystic Sheikh Moinuddin Chishti and made several pilgrimages to his shrine at Ajmer. He craved religious unity of his people and with that vision founded the sect Din-i-Ilahi (Faith of the Divine). Din-i-Ilahi was in essence an ethical system that dictated the preferred way of life discarding qualities like lust, slander and pride. It borrowed heavily from existing religions extracting the best philosophies and forming an amalgamation of virtues to live by.

Architecture and Culture

Akbar commissioned the building of several forts and mausoleums during his reign and established a distinct architectural style that has been dubbed as Mughal architecture by connoisseurs. Among the architectural marvels commissioned during his rule are the Agra Fort (1565–1574), the town of Fatehpur Sikri (1569–1574) with its beautiful Jami Masjid and Buland Darwaza, Humayun's Tomb (1565-1572), Ajmer Fort (1563-1573), Lahore Fort (1586-1618) and Allahabad Fort (1583-1584).

Akbar was a great patron of art and culture. Although he himself could not read and write, he would appoint people who read to him various topics of art, history, philosophy and religion. He appreciated intellectual discourse and offered his patronage to several extraordinarily talented people whom he invited to his court. Together these individuals were referred to as the Nava Ratnas or the Nine Gems. They were Abul Fazel, Faizi, Mian Tansen, Birbal, Raja Todar Mal, Raja Man Singh, Abdul Rahim Khan-I-Khana , Fakir Aziao-Din and Mullah Do Piaza. They came from various backgrounds and were revered by the emperor for their special talents.

Death of Akbar

In 1605, at the age of 63, Akbar fell ill with a serious case of dysentery. He never recovered from it and after three weeks of suffering, he passed away on October 27, 1605 at Fatehpur Sikri. He was buried at Sikandra, Agra.

IV
Jahangir

Jahangir : Fourth Mughal Emperor

Original Name: Mirza Nur-ud-din Beig Mohammad Khan Salim
Birth: 31 August 1569
Place of Birth: Fatehpur Sikri, Mughal Empire
Coronation: 24 November 1605
Reign: 3 November 1605 – 28 October 1627
Death: 28 October 1627
Place of Death: Rajauri, Kashmir, Mughal Empire
Father: Akbar the Great
Mother: Mariam-uz-Zamani

Consort: Nur Jahan
Predecessor: Akbar
Successor: Shahryar Mirza, Shah Jahan
Wives: Nur Jahan, Shah Begum, Jagat Gosain, Sahib Jamal, Malika Jahan, Nur-un-Nisa Begum, Khas Mahal, Karamsi, Saliha Banu Begum
Children: Khusrau Mirza, Parviz Mirza, Khurram Mirza, Shahryar Mirza, Jahandar Mirza, Sultan-un-Nissa Begum, Daulat-un-Nissa Begum, Bahar Banu Begum, Begum Sultan Begum, Iffat Banu Begum

Jahangir was the fourth Mughal emperor and one of the most prominent rulers of the great empire. He ruled from 1605 until his death in 1627. He had a bitter relationship with his father and tried to revolt against Akbar several times, but the father and son later reconciled. Apart from his military campaigns, Jahangir also gave importance to arts, especially painting. Jehangir's relationship with the Mughal courtesan, Anarkali, has been the subject of several films and literature pieces. He also ordered the execution of the fifth Sikh Guru, Guru Arjan Dev. By 1627, Jahangir's health had deteriorated, and he died on October 28, 1627. His mausoleum, Tomb of Jahangir, located at Shahdara, is a major tourist attraction in present-day Lahore.

Childhood & Early Life

Jahangir was born Nur-ud-din Muhammad Salim on August 31, 1569, at Fatehpur Sikri, Mughal Empire, in present-day Uttar Pradesh. Since Mughal Emperor Akbar's previous children had died at various stages of infancy, Akbar had become increasingly worried and hence approached a few holy men to bless him and his wife Mariam-uz-Zamani (Jodha Bai) with a son. The royal couple was subsequently blessed with a son, whom they named Salim. He was named after a Sufi saint, Salim Chishti, who had earlier blessed Akbar.

As a young prince, Jahangir had rebelled against his father for various reasons, including the throne. Upon Akbar's death on October 27, 1605, Jahangir ascended the throne forcefully, which did not go down well with many within the royal court. In fact, his own son, Khusrau Mirza, had revolted against him. Mirza had claimed that he was the rightful heir to the Mughal throne as per his grandfather Akbar's wish. But when his father crowned himself the emperor, Mirza became rebellious and chose to fight against Jahangir.

Jahangir's forces were successful in defeating Khusrau Mirza and his supporters in the battle of Bhairowal. Khusrau and his supporters were caught by Jahangir's men and brought to Delhi. Despite being the emperor's son, Khusrau Mirza was partially blinded for his act of treason. He was later killed on January 26, 1622, at the orders of his brother, Prince Khurram (Shah Jahan), who was Jahangir's favorite.

Marriages

Jahangir had a total of 20 wives, including his favorite wife and consort, Nur Jahan. Many of his weddings were conducted for political reasons, while others were personal. In 1585, when Jahangir was barely 16 years old, he was engaged to the Rajput princess of Amer, Man Bai. Man Bai was Jahangir's cousin as his mother, Jodha Bai, was related to Man Bai's father. The wedding took place on February 13, 1585, post which the couple was blessed with two children. At the time of their son Khusrau Mirza's birth, Jahangir changed Man Bai's name to Shah Begum (royal lady).

After his first wedding, Jahangir married few other women in quick succession. On June 26, 1586, Jahangir married Udai Singh's daughter, Jagat Gosain. The wedding was a political event as Udai Singh had promised to give his daughter's hand in marriage to Jahangir after accepting Akbar's suzerainty. Jagat Gosain, who was known for her beauty, intelligence, courage, and wit, became Jahangir's favorite wife soon after their wedding. The couple was blessed with three children, including two daughters, who had died in infancy. Their only son, Khurram, who would later ascend the throne as Emperor Shah Jahan, became Jahangir's favorite son.

After marrying the daughter of Raja Rai Singh of Bikaner on July 7, 1586, he went on to marry Malika Shikar Begum, the princess of Kashghar in the same month. In October 1586, he married Sahib Jamal. Sahib Jamal gave birth to two children – a son named Sultan Parviz Mirza and a daughter who died young. In 1587, he married the Rajput princess of Jaisalmer, Malika Jahan.

In October 1590, he married Mirza Sanjar Hazara's daughter, Zohra Begum. The following year, he married Karamnasi Begum, the princess of Mertia. He then married Kanwal Rani on January 11, 1592, and then followed it up with another marriage with the daughter of Husain Chak of Kashmir on October 1592. By 1596, Jahangir had married three other women and had fallen in love with Khas Mahal Begum. On June 28, 1596, Jahangir married Khas Mahal, who became the empress when Jahangir ascended the throne.

After marrying Saliha Banu Begum in 1608, Jahangir married the daughter of Prince Jagat Singh, Koka Kumari Begum on June 17, 1608. After marrying a few more women in subsequent years, he married Mehr-un-Nisaa (Nur Jahan), who became his twentieth and last wife. Nur Jahan went on to become Jahangir's favorite wife, so much so that she had control over the entire empire during her reign as the emperor's royal consort.

Marriage with Nur Jahan & Her Influence

Mehr-un-Nisaa, who later came to be known as Nur Jahan, was married to Sher Afgan Khan. According to certain texts, Jahangir was attracted to Mehr-un-Nisaa even when she was already married to Sher Afgan Khan. Since she was a beautiful, strong, witty, well-educated, and a charismatic woman, Jahangir had fallen head over heels in love with her. Soon after Sher Afgan's death, Jahangir summoned Mehr-un-Nissa to Agra. In 1611, four years after the death of Sher Afgan, Emperor Jahangir proposed to Mehr-un-Nissa during the festival of 'Nowruz.' Jahangir married her on May 25, 1611, and bestowed upon her the title 'Nur Mahal.' Five years later, she was honored with the title of 'Nur Jahan,' which translates to 'Light of the World.'

After her wedding with Jahangir, Nur Jahan became his favorite wife and had his complete attention. As a result, she wielded influence over the administration of the Mughal Empire and was considered very powerful at the court. She had great influence on Jahangir and thereby had a direct influence on the affairs of the state. She was actively involved in political and military affairs and even held independent courts whenever required. Simply put, she became the power behind the Mughal throne during Jahangir's reign. Nur Jahan also possessed great administrative skills and bravery, which she used to defend the Empire's borders at the time of Jahangir's absence. She was also known for her ability to lead armed forces whenever required.

Conquests

While most north Indian territories were conquered by Jahangir's father, Akbar, some regions including Mewar in Rajasthan were left unconquered by Akbar. Also, Akbar had failed to capture regions in South India. After becoming the emperor, Jahangir's primary goal was to capture areas unconquered by Akbar. Hence, Jahangir's first military campaign was against Rana Amar Singh of Mewar. Almost immediately after becoming the emperor, Jahangir sent an expedition headed by Parwez to conquer Mewar. However, the contingent was recalled when his son, Khusrau Mirza, rose in revolt against him. After defeating Khusrau Mirza, Jahangir sent another expedition to Mewar. This time around, he was successful in making Rana Amar Singh of Mewar surrender before him, which led to a peace treaty between Rana and Jahangir. The peace treaty, which was signed in 1615, was favorable to the Mughals.

After gaining control over Mewar, Jahangir turned his attention towards South India. While trying to conquer Ahmednagar, Jahangir was confronted by Malik Ambar, the Wazir of Ahmednagar. Despite his best efforts, Jahangir was not able to gain complete control over regions like Ahmednagar, Golconda, and Bijapur. However, the king of Bijapur acted as a mediator between the ruler of Ahmednagar and the Mughals. Subsequently the ruler of Bijapur succeeded in arranging a peace treaty between Ahmednagar and the Mughal Empire, post which a few forts and the territory of Balaghat were given to the Mughals. But Malik Ambar did not abide by the rules of the treaty and besieged the Ahmednagar fort in 1620. In 1621, another peace treaty was signed between Malik Ambar and the Mughals, post which the ruler of Ahmednagar surrendered the territories he had earlier captured from the Mughals. The Mughals were also awarded monetary compensation as a result of the treaty. However, Jahangir could never gain complete control over South India, which makes the treaty of Mewar his best military event.

Death

By 1627, Jahangir's heath had deteriorated, which prompted him to visit places like Kashmir and Kabul with the hope of restoring his health. After visiting Kashmir, the emperor decided to return to Lahore as his health worsened due to severe cold. While returning to Lahore along with his contingent, Jahangir passed away on October 28, 1627, at Sarai Saadabad in Bhimber. After removing his entrails, his body was temporarily buried in Baghsar Fort and was later moved to Lahore, where it was buried in Shahdara Bagh. His mausoleum, Tomb of Jahangir, which is located at Shahdara, is a major tourist attraction in present-day Lahore.

Religious Views

Though he was not a religious person, a statement which is often confused by the westerners, who say that he was an atheist, Jahangir observed the principles of Islam as he had faith in God. When it came to handling his subjects, Jahangir did not grant special and biased powers to Muslims, nor did he burden the Hindus with special taxes. However, he is said to have tortured many Hindus for marrying Muslim girls in Kashmir. Interestingly, the emperor himself married many Hindu women, which left them with no other option but to convert to Islam.

Jahangir's hatred towards the fifth Sikh Guru, Guru Arjan Dev, paved the way for tension between the Sikhs and the Mughals for a very long time. Though seen as a political move by many, Jahangir's decision to execute Guru Arjan Dev convinced people that Jahangir hated Hindus and the Sikhs. In another instance, Jahangir is said to have ordered the removal of a Varaha statue while visiting a Hindu temple. These incidents are viewed as evidences of Jahangir's dislike towards other religions, especially Hinduism.

Jahangir was attracted by Christian themes, which played a major role in him allowing the British to conduct trade in his territory. In fact, many texts suggest that Jahangir had pictures of Christ in his prayer room. It is also said that the Mughal emperor had pictures of angels and demons, with demons portrayed as ugly creatures. Jahangir's liking towards Christianity was so great that there were rumors that suggested he had converted to Christianity. However, these rumors were rubbished by the English ambassador, Thomas Roe, who could not figure out Jahangir's intention towards other religions.

Art During Jahangir's Reign

Apart from strengthening his military prowess, Jahangir also gave importance to arts, especially painting. During his reign, the emperor commissioned many paintings, including several portraits of himself. The Mughal painting flourished under Jahangir's reign, which provided opportunity to many artists. He also carefully preserved paintings, which were commissioned by his father, Akbar. Jahangir was greatly influenced by European art and architecture. According to English ambassador, Thomas Roe, the emperor would have his court painters reproduce a European miniature and then would challenge Thomas Roe to pick the original work. Whenever Roe failed to pick the original work, Jahangir would derive immense satisfaction and pride from it. The 'British Museum' in London has a collection of 74 paintings that were commissioned by Jahangir. Like many other Mughal emperors, Jahangir too, encouraged art and welcomed artists from across the world to exhibit their talent in the Mughal court.

V
Shah Jahan

Shah Jahan : Creator of Tajmahal

Date of Birth: January 5, 1592
Place of Birth: Lahore, Pakistan
Birth Name: Shahab-ud-din Muhammad Khurram
Date of Death: January 22, 1666
Place of Death: Agra, India

Reign: January 19, 1628 to July 31, 1658

Spouses: Kandahari Mahal, Akbarabadi Mahal, Mumtaz Mahal, Fatehpuri Mahal, Muti Begum

Children: Aurangzeb, Dara Shukoh, Jahanara Begum, Shah Shuja, Murad Bakhsh, Roshanara Begum, Gauhara Begum, Parhez Banu Begum, Husnara Begum, Sultan Luftallah, Sultan Daulat Afza, Huralnissa Begum, Shahzadi Surayya Banu Begum, Sultan Ummid Baksh

Father:Jahangir

Mother: Jagat Gosaini

Shah Jahan (Shahab-ud-din Muhammad Khurram) was one of the most successful emperors of the Mughal Empire. He was the fifth Mughal ruler after Babur, Humayun, Akbar and Jahangir. After winning the war of succession post the demise of his father Jahangir, Shah Jahan successfully ruled the empire for 30 years. During his reign, the Mughal Empire thrived, making his reign the golden era of the empire. Though Shah Jahan was an able administrator and commander, he is best known for the construction of the Taj Mahal, which he built in the memory of his beloved wife, Mumtaz Mahal. Architecture in general saw the best of Mughal construction during his time. He is credited with constructing many beautiful monuments throughout the landscape of North India. Shah Jahan is also the founder of Shahjahanabad in Delhi. The exquisite 'Peacock Throne', which he got built for himself, is believed to be worth millions of dollars by modern estimates. During his final days, he was held captive by his son Aurangzeb, who went on to succeed him to the throne.

Legend Associated With His Birth

Emperor Akbar's first wife Ruqaiya Sultan Begum was childless throughout her marriage. Though she couldn't give birth to a royal prince or princess, she was told by a fortune teller that she would be responsible in raising a future Emperor. The prediction was such that Akbar's favorite grandson, who would go on to become the the fifth Mughal Emperor, would be brought up by the childless Empress. So, when Jahangir's third son was born, Akbar instinctively knew that he would be raised by his childless Empress.

Childhood

As per the prediction of the fortune teller, Shah Jahan was born on 5thJanuary 1592, to Emperor Jahangir and his second wife, Jagat Gosaini (a Rajput princess). After naming him Khurram (the joyous one), his grandfather, Emperor Akbar took him away from his mother and handed him over to his Empress Ruqaiya Sultan Begum. Khurram, who was just six days old, started growing up under the care of Akbar and Ruqaiya Sultan Begum.

Quite naturally, young Khurram was fond of Akbar and his foster mother more than his biological parents. Ruqaiya Sultan Begum raised him with love and care and made that her top priority. In fact, Jahangir once famously said that he (Khurram) was showered with more love by Ruqaiya Sultan Begum than he or his wife ever could have. He received a traditional princely education that involved training in martial arts and cultural arts which included music and poetry.While Akbar would instill in him the different techniques of warfare and leadership, his foster mother would narrate him the importance of moral values. In 1605, post the demise of Akbar, a 13-year-old Khurram returned to his biological parents.

Engagement With Mumtaz Mahal

In 1607, the 15-year-old Khurram got engaged to Arjumand Banu Begum (Mumtaz Mahal). However, the court astrologers had predicted that the couple should not marry until 1612, for their marriage wouldn't be pleasant otherwise. Paying heed to the astrologers, Khurram's parents and well-wishers decided to put off his wedding with Mumtaz until 1612, making the couple wait for another five years.

Khurram's Weddings

After he was told to wait until 1612 for his wedding with Mumtaz, Khurram went ahead with his first wedding with Kandahari Begum, a princess from Persia. He had his first child, a daughter, with her. He then married another princess before marrying Mumtaz Mahal in 1612. After having fathered two children from his first two marriages, he fathered fourteen children with his favorite wife Mumtaz. He also married two other women namely Akbarabadi Mahal and Muti Begum, but it is said that these marriages were for political reasons and the women he married for such reasons were considered more as 'royal wives.'

Road to Throne (Part 1)

The accession to the throne in the Mughal Empire was determined through military successes and display of power by potential successors. The Mughal had stayed away from the traditional primogeniture method of choosing the rightful heir and that made Khurram a potential successor to Jahangir, even though he was the third child of the emperor. In 1614, Khurram got an opportunity to display his military prowess, something he was so desperately waiting for.The moment he was waiting to seize came in the form of Maharana Amar Singh II, who was asked to surrender his Rajput state to the Mughal. Khurram led an army of more than 200,000 men and defeated the forces of the Rajput king. This brave act of his, paved the way for moresuch opportunities. Three years later in 1617, he was asked to conquer the Deccan Plateau in order to expand the empire. After his success in doing so, his father Jahangir bestowed upon him the title Shah Jahan, which literally meant King of the World in Persian. This made him the blue-eyed boy of the empire and his dream of succeeding his father strode a step closer to reality.

Road to Throne (Part 2)

Though Shah Jahan had proved his abilities and prowess more than once, the fight for the throne was harder than he thought it would be. Jahangir married Nur Jahan and she along with her brother Asaf Khan, became important members in the court. Also, Nur Jahan got her daughter (from first marriage) married to Shahzada Shahryar, Shah Jahan's younger brother. She then continued to convince the emperor that Shahzada Shahryar was better than Shah Jahan and that he should be the one to succeed him. This led a rebellious Shah Jahan to build his own army with the help of a Mughal general named Mahabat Khan. He then led his army against his own father and Nur Jahan but was defeated comprehensively in the year 1623. Three years later, he was forgiven by the emperor but Shah Jahan continued to find ways which would lead him to the throne. In 1627, upon the demise of Jahangir, Shah Jahan crowned himself emperor as the entire military was under his control.

Overcoming The Opposition

As soon as he became the emperor, Shah Jahan eliminated all his foes just to make sure the throne had no further contenders. He killed many in the year 1628 including his brother Shahzada Shahryar; his cousins, Tahmuras and Hoshang; his nephews, Garshasp and Dawar, and sons of prince Daniyal and prince Khusrau. Anyone he thought would be a threat to his throne was put to rest permanently. His step-mother Nur Jahan was spared but was imprisoned under tight security.

Shah Jahan's Reign

Throughout his reign, Shah Jahan constantly strived towards expanding his empire. This gave rise to many battles and some alliances. While he joined hands with some of the Rajput kings of Bundelkhand, Baglana and Mewar, he waged war on the others like the Bundela Rajputs. In 1632, he captured the fortress at Daulatabad and imprisoned Husain Shah. He appointed his son Aurangzeb as his Viceroy who in turn captured places like Golconda and Bijapur of South India. He then went on to capture Kandahar, which led to the famous Mughal–Safavid War. His empire now stretched beyond Khyber Pass and all the way to Ghazna.

Shah Jahan's Army

Shah Jahan invested most of his time in building a massive army. It is said that his army included more than 911,400 soldiers and 185,000 horsemen. He was also responsible in manufacturing cannonsin huge numbers.

During his 30 year reign, Shah Jahan transformedhis empire into a well-oiled military machine.

Contribution to Mughal Architecture

Shah Jahan was an avid builder and is responsible for building some of the most beautiful edifices in present day India and Pakistan. It is said that many European travelers would visit his empire just to learn the different techniques used in the construction of buildings. It is also said that some of the world's most talented engineers and architects resided in his empire.

Construction of The Taj Mahal

One of the most significant incidents in the life of Mughal Emperor Shah Jahan was the construction of Taj Mahal. His beloved wife Mumtaz Mahal died while giving birth to their fourteenth child and the reason behind her death was stated to be postpartum haemorrhage. This left Shah Jahan devastated who then decided to build the world's most beautiful monument in the memory of his wife. After many years of planning, hard work and immense sacrifices, the monument, which came to be known as the Taj Mahal was built.Today people from different parts of the world travel to India just to see this amazing white colored edifice which is also one of the most visited tourist destinations of India. Taj Mahal continues to beone of the Seven Wonders of the World!

Other Structures Built by Shah Jahan

The following monuments were also constructed by Shah Jahan during his rule:

- Red Fort or Lal Quila (Delhi)
- Sections of the Agra Fort
- Jama Masjid (Delhi)
- Moti Masjid or Pearl Mosque (Lahore)
- Shalimar Gardens (Lahore)
- Sections of the Lahore Fort (Lahore)
- Jahangir Mausoleum
- Takht-e-Taus

Shahjahan Mosque (Thatta)

Taj Mahal

Final Days

Shah Jahan became seriously ill in September 1658. During his days of recovery, Dara Shikoh, one of his sons, assumed the role of the ruler. This made his brothers furious and almost immediately, Shuja and Murad Baksh sought independent provinces and claimed their rightful share. Meanwhile, Aurangzeb had formed an army of his own and went on to defeat his brother Dara Shikoh. He then killed rest of the contenders and declared himself as the emperor. Though Shah Jahan later recovered from his illness, Aurangzeb deemed him unfit to rule and imprisoned him in the citadel of Agra. He also imprisoned his sister Jahanara Begum Sahib who wanted to stay with her father in order to take care of him. Shah Jahan is said to have spent eight long years of his imprisonment by staring at the tomb of his beloved wife – the marvel that he built in her memory.

Death

In the first week of January 1666, Shah Jahan once again fell ill and never recovered. On January 22, he is said to have summoned Akbarabadi Mahal and requested her to take care of his daughter, Jahanara Begum. He is then said to have recited a few lines from the holy Quran before breathing his last, aged 74. The emperor who once ruled the whole of India and more had died a prisoner. Princess Jahanara Begum wanted a procession with the state's noblemen carrying her father's body all over Agra so that the subjects could waive a final goodbye to their beloved emperor. However, Aurangzeb was in no mood for such an extravagant funeral. In the end, Sayyid Muhammad Qanauji and Kazi Qurban moved the body of Shah Jahan out of the prison, washed it and placed it in a coffin made out of sandalwood. The coffin was then brought to the Taj Mahal through the river, where he was laid to rest, next to his beloved wife, Mumtaz.

Shah jahan with his beloved wife Mumtaj mahal

SHIVAM

VI
Aurangzeb

Aurangzeb : 6th Mughal Emperor

Aurangzeb, also spelled Aurangzib, Arabic Awrangzīb, kingly title
ʿĀlamgīr, original name Muḥī al-Dīn Muḥammad, (born November 3, 1618,
Dhod, Malwa [India]—died March 3, 1707), emperor of India from 1658 to
1707, the last of the great Mughal emperors. Under him the Mughal Empire
reached its greatest extent, although his policies helped lead to its

dissolution.

- **Known For**: Emperor of India
- **Also Known As**: Muhi-ud-Din Muhammad, Alamgir
- **Born**: November 3, 1618 in Dahod, India
- **Parents**: Shah Jahan, Mumtaz Mahal
- **Died**: March 3, 1707 in Bhingar, Ahmednagar, India
- **Spouse(s)**: Nawab Bai, Dilras Banu Begum, Aurangabadi Mahal
- **Children**: Zeb-un-Nissa, Muhammad Sultan, Zinat-un-Nissa, Bahadur Shah I, Badr-un-Nissa, Zubdat-un-Nissa, Muhammad Azam Shah, Sultan Muhammad Akbar, Mehr-un-Nissa, Muhammad Kam Bakhsh
- **Notable Quote**: "Strange, that I came into the world with nothing, and now I am going away with this stupendous caravan of sin! Wherever I look, I see only God...I have sinned terribly, and I do not know what punishment awaits me." (supposedly communicated on his deathbed)

Early life

Aurangzeb was the third son of the emperor Shah Jahān and Mumtaz Mahal (for whom the Taj Mahal was built). He grew up as a serious-minded and devout youth, wedded to the Muslim orthodoxy of the day and free from the royal Mughal traits of sensuality and drunkenness. He showed signs of military and administrative ability early; these qualities, combined with a taste for power, brought him into rivalry with his eldest brother, the brilliant and volatile Dārā Shikōh, who was designated by their father as his successor to the throne. From 1636 Aurangzeb held a number of important appointments, in all of which he distinguished himself. He commanded troops against the Uzbeks and the Persians with distinction (1646–47) and, as viceroy of the Deccan provinces in two terms (1636–44, 1654–58), reduced the two Muslim Deccan kingdoms to near-subjection.

When Shah Jahān fell seriously ill in 1657, the tension between the two brothers made a war of succession seem inevitable. By the time of Shah Jahān's unexpected recovery, matters had gone too far for either son to retreat. In the struggle for power (1657–59), Aurangzeb showed tactical and strategic military skill, great powers of dissimulation, and ruthless determination. Decisively defeating Dārā at Samugarh in May 1658, he confined his father in his own palace at Agra. In consolidating his power,

Aurangzeb caused one brother's death and had two other brothers, a son, and a nephew executed.

Emperor of India

Aurangzeb's reign falls into two almost equal parts. In the first, which lasted until about 1680, he was a capable Muslim monarch of a mixed Hindu-Muslim empire and as such was generally disliked for his ruthlessness but feared and respected for his vigour and skill. During this period he was much occupied with safeguarding the northwest from Persians and Central Asian Turks and less so with the Maratha chief Shivaji, who twice plundered the great port of Surat (1664, 1670). Aurangzeb applied his great-grandfather Akbar's recipe for conquest: defeat one's enemies, reconcile them, and place them in imperial service. Thus, Shivaji was defeated, called to Agra for reconciliation (1666), and given an imperial rank. The plan broke down, however; Shivaji fled to the Deccan and died, in 1680, as the ruler of an independent Maratha kingdom.

After about 1680, Aurangzeb's reign underwent a change of both attitude and policy. The pious ruler of an Islamic state replaced the seasoned statesman of a mixed kingdom; Hindus became subordinates, not colleagues, and the Marathas, like the southern Muslim kingdoms, were marked for annexation rather than containment. The first overt sign of change was the reimposition of the jizya, or poll tax, on non-Muslims in 1679 (a tax that had been abolished by Akbar). This in turn was followed by a Rajput revolt in 1680–81, supported by Aurangzeb's third son, Akbar. Hindus still served the empire, but no longer with enthusiasm. The Deccan kingdoms of Bijapur and Golconda were conquered in 1686–87, but the insecurity that followed precipitated a long-incipient economic crisis, which in turn was deepened by warfare with the Marathas. Shivaji's son Sambhaji was captured and executed in 1689 and his kingdom broken up. The Marathas, however, then adopted guerrilla tactics, spreading all over southern India amid a sympathetic population. The rest of Aurangzeb's life was spent in laborious and fruitless sieges of forts in the Maratha hill country.

Aurangzeb's absence in the south prevented him from maintaining his former firm hold on the north. The administration weakened, and the process was hastened by pressure on the land by Mughal grantees who were paid by assignments on the land revenue. Agrarian discontent often took the form of religious movements, as in the case of the Satnamis and the Sikhs in the Punjab. In 1675 Aurangzeb arrested and executed the Sikh Guru (spiritual leader) Tegh Bahadur, who had refused to embrace Islam; the succeeding Guru, Gobind Singh, was in open rebellion for the rest of Aurangzeb's reign. Other agrarian revolts, such as those of the Jats, were largely secular.

In general, Aurangzeb ruled as a militant orthodox Sunni Muslim; he put through increasingly puritanical ordinances that were vigorously enforced by muḥtasibs, or censors of morals. The Muslim confession of faith, for instance, was removed from all coins lest it be defiled by unbelievers, and courtiers were forbidden to salute in the Hindu fashion. In addition, Hindu idols, temples, and shrines were often destroyed.

Aurangzeb maintained the empire for nearly half a century and in fact extended it in the south as far as Tanjore (now Thanjavur) and Trichinopoly (now Tiruchchirappalli). Behind this imposing facade, however, were serious weaknesses. The Maratha campaign continually drained the imperial resources. The militancy of the Sikhs and the Jats boded ill for the empire in the north. The new Islamic policy alienated Hindu sentiment and undermined Rajput support. The financial pressure on the land strained the whole administrative framework. When Aurangzeb died after a reign of nearly 49 years, he left an empire not yet moribund but confronted with a number of menacing problems. The failure of the Mughals to cope with them after the reign of his son Bahādur Shāh I led to the collapse of the empire in the mid-18th century.

EnLahore, Pakistan: Badshahi (Imperial) MosqueBadshahi (Imperial) Mosque, one of Aurangzeb's architectural achievements, in Lahore, Pakistan.ter Caption

Bahadur Shah zafar ll

Bahadur Shah zafar ll : the last Mughal emperor of India

Bahādur Shāh II, also called Bahādur Shāh Ẓafar, (born October 24, 1775, Delhi, India—died November 7, 1862, Rangoon [now Yangon], Myanmar), the last Mughal emperor of India (reigned 1837–57). He was a poet, musician, and calligrapher, more an aesthete than a political leader.

He was the second son of Akbar Shāh II and Lāl Bāī. For most of his reign he was a client of the British and was without real authority. He figured briefly, and reluctantly, in the Indian Mutiny of 1857–58; during the mutiny, rebel troops from the city of Meerut seized Delhi and compelled Bahādur Shāh to accept nominal leadership of the revolt. He was arrested by the British Army after it captured Delhi in September 1857. After the rebellion was put down by the British, he was tried and exiled to Burma (Myanmar) with his family.

THE DAY OF THE REVOLT

On the morning of 11 May 1857, Delhi and various other parts of the country were convulsed by a rebellion. When the revolutionaries approached him, being an innately sensitive person he was reluctant to lead them. Nevertheless, he did agree to become the leader of the Revolt of 1857. Soon, the revolt that had spread to other cities in North India was crushed by British troops.

In Delhi, under the command of General Nicholson, the first three columns gathered in and behind Qudsia Bagh, a former summer residence of the Mughal Emperors. The fourth column was intended to attack only when the Kabul Gate on the west of the city walls was opened by the other columns. The fifth column and the cavalry were in reserve.

The third column attacked Kashmiri Gate on the north wall. Many British soldeirs were wounded and killed. The explosion demolished a part of the gate. Meanwhile, the fourth column encountered a rebel force outside the Kabul Gate before the other columns attacked and were thrown into disarray. This confrontation led to heavy casualties, leading to Nicholson's death.

The British later moved to the Church of Saint James, just inside the walls of the Kashmir Bastion. They had suffered 1,170 casualties according to intelligence reports.

CAPTURE OF ZAFAR AND THE ROYAL FAMILY

The outbreak of the revolt in Delhi in May culminated in the final British clamp down on the Mughal rule. On 19th September 1857, Red Fort was captured. The King, along with the other members of the Royal family had already fled to Humayun's Tomb for refuge.

On 21ˢᵗ September, due to the exertions of Major William Hodson and his intelligencer, Maulvi Rajab Ali, Bahadur Shah Zafar surrendered on the condition that his life and that of his wife, Zinat Mahal will be spared. The very same day, he was taken prisoner by Hodson.

The British confined him in the house of Zinat Mahal in Lal Kuan under the supervision of a European guard and made it clear that he will not be entitled to any royal treatment because of his former designation. Rather, he would be guarded according to his present position of a prisoner.

The very next day, Hodson and his cavalry again surrounded Humayun's Tomb and captured two sons of the King, Mirza Mughal, Mirza Khizr Sultan and his grandson, Mirza Abu Bakr, "all of whom had been prominent in the insurrections." They were made prisoners and shot in cold-blood by Hodson at a location (today known as Khooni Darwaza or the Gate of Blood) near the Delhi Gate. W. Muir, in-charge of the Intelligence Department wrote, "their bodies are now lying at the Kotwali where so many of our poor countrymen were murdered and exposed."

Simultaneously, the British were also carrying a heartless rampage in Delhi. On 14ᵗʰ September 1857, Delhi was assaulted and by the 20ᵗʰ was captured by the British.

EXILE

With the fear that the descendants of Zafar in future might challenge the British authority, they decided to deport the royal family to a distant place and keep them under surveillance.

They also proposed that, "the entire expatriation of the whole race, whether innocent or guilty without distinction of age so that there may not remain or arise in India a single person to whom the disaffected can point as the representative of the Mahomedan dynasty."

Bahadur Shah Zafar was 83 years old when he arrived in Rangoon. During his stay there, his health declined further. He had developed paralysis in the throat region and finally succumbed to it on 7 November 1862. He was buried in an anonymous grave.